Indira
GANDHI

ANITA GANERI

Heinemann Library
Chicago, Illinois

© 2003 Heinemann Library
a division of Reed Elsevier Inc.
Chicago, Illinois

Customer Service 888-454-2279

Visit our website at www.heinemannlibrary.com

Originated by Dot Gradations, Ltd.
Printed by South China Printing Company, Ltd.

07 06 05 04 03
10 9 8 7 6 5 4 3 2 1

Library of Congress Cataloging-in-Publication Data
Ganeri, Anita.
   Indira Gandhi / Anita Ganeri.
      p. cm. -- (Leading lives)
Summary: Examines the life of Indira Gandhi, the first woman prime minister of India, and her impact on the politics of her country.
Includes bibliographical references and index.
   ISBN 1-40340-833-5 (HC)
   1. Gandhi, Indira, 1917-1984--Juvenile literature. 2. Women prime ministers--India--Biography--Juvenile literature. 3. India--Politics and government--20th century. [1. Gandhi, Indira, 1917-1984. 2. Prime ministers. 3. Women--Biography. 4. India--Politics and government--20th century.] I. Title. II. Series.
   DS481.G23 G25 2002
   954.04'5'092--dc21

2002012043

Acknowledgements
The author and publishers are grateful to the following for permission to reproduce copyright material: pp. 4, 37, 43, 52, 54 Popperfoto; pp. 6, 9, 11, 17, 20, 25, 29, 32, 35, 36 Getty Images; pp. 14, 24, 28, 40, 41, 45, 46, 50, 55 Bettmann/Corbis; pp. 22, 38 Hulton-Deutsch Collection/Corbis; pp. 31, 49, 51 Topham/Associated Press; pp. 34, 53 Topham Picturepoint; p. 48 Corbis.

Cover photograph of Indira Gandhi reproduced with permission of Corbis.

Some words are shown in bold, **like this.** You can find out what they mean by looking in the glossary.

Contents

1 A New Leader for India

On a cold and misty January day in Delhi, the capital of India, in the central hall of the Indian **parliament,** the **Congress Party** has gathered to elect a new leader—and to witness the making of history. Excitement crackles in the air. This leader will serve not only as leader of the Congress Party, but also as **prime minister** of India and head of the world's largest **democracy.**

▲ *Indira Gandhi is sworn in as the first woman prime minister of India.*

As the members of parliament (MPs) cast their votes, a tall, slender woman with dark, brooding eyes watches intently. She is Indira Gandhi (1917–1984), the front-running candidate. Indira wears a simple white, robelike dress called a **khadi sari** and a plain shawl. She has draped a string of brown beads around her neck. The beads are her lucky charm, given to her long before by a **Hindu** holy woman. Someone has presented her with a bouquet of roses, and now one of them is pinned to her sari. At last, election officials count the votes. Indira has beaten her closest rival, 355 votes to 169. In five days, the government will swear her in as the first woman prime minister of India.

To locate the places mentioned, see the map of India on page 30.

As the daughter of Jawaharlal Nehru, India's first prime minister, Indira has lived her whole life in the political spotlight. She took part in the final years of India's struggle for independence from almost 100 years of British rule. Later, she acted as her father's constant companion. She has seen most of her family jailed as they helped to fight for independence. She has even spent time in prison herself. But now how will she handle the enormous task that lies ahead? After all, it is extremely rare for a woman to become a politician in India, where men hold all the power. How will she tackle the problems of poverty and **corruption** that the country faces? And what about the fighting between the different religious groups of India that threatens to tear the country apart?

FOR DETAILS ON KEY PEOPLE OF INDIRA GANDHI'S TIME, SEE PAGE 58.

First words as prime minister

"My heart is full and I do not know how to thank you. As I stand before you my thoughts go back to the great leaders: [Mohandas] Gandhi [the independence leader], at whose feet I grew up, Panditji [Jawaharlal Nehru], my father, and Lal Bahadur Shastri [the second prime minister of India]. These leaders have shown the way, and I want to go along the same path."

(Indira Gandhi, on becoming prime minister of India, 1966)

These issues hover on the horizon. For now, nothing can spoil her moment of triumph. As she leaves parliament, a cheering crowd greets her. "Indira Gandhi zindabad!" they shout. "Long live Indira Gandhi!" Indira Gandhi is about to become one of the most powerful women in the world.

2 | Birth and Family

TO LOCATE THE PLACES MENTIONED, SEE THE MAP OF INDIA ON PAGE 30.

Indira Priyadarshini Nehru was born on November 19, 1917, in the bustling city of Allahabad, in northern India. She was the only child of Jawaharlal Nehru, future **prime minister** of India, and his wife Kamala. Some of the Nehru women could

▼ *Jawaharlal Nehru, Indira's father, poses as a boy for a family photo with his parents Swaruprani and Motilal.*

not hide their disappointment that Indira was not a boy. In traditional Indian society, boys were all-important for caring for their parents and carrying on the family name. But these remarks irritated Indira's grandfather, Motilal. "This daughter of Jawaharlal, for all you know," he said angrily, "may prove better than a thousand sons."

The Nehrus

The remarkable Nehru family, into which Indira—or Indu, as people called her then—was born, was an upper-class **Hindu** family whose **ancestors** came from Kashmir. The head of the family, Motilal Nehru, was one of Allahabad's most brilliant and respected lawyers. Like the rest of the household, Indu's grandfather awed her. He could be impatient and quick-tempered, but she adored him and he, in turn, spoiled her. She later wrote: "I was tremendously impressed by my grandfather's bigness. I don't mean physically—but you know, he seemed to embrace the whole world. I loved the way he laughed."

Indu's grandfather firmly believed in the advantages of a good education for girls and boys alike. This was unusual because in India at that time, usually only boys received an education. Girls stayed at home and helped their mothers run the household. Governesses educated Motilal's daughters at home and his only son Jawaharlal Nehru attended school and college in England. On his return to India, Jawaharlal joined his father's law practice. Later, both Motilal and Jawaharlal became leaders in the struggle for India's independence from British rule. From early childhood, Indu's father's and grandfather's strong political views greatly influenced her.

The other members of the Nehru household included Indira's grandmother, Swaruprani; Swaruprani's widowed sister, Bibi Amma; Indira's two aunts, Vijayalakshmi and Krishna; and her mother Kamala. In addition, servants took care of the family and various other friends and relatives were always coming to stay. In total, the household numbered nearly 100 people.

House of happiness

Indira was born in Motilal's magnificent mansion, Anand Bhavan. The name means House of Happiness in the **Hindi** language. The huge, rambling house had 42 rooms surrounded by balconies, and a decorative dome stood on top of it. From the viewing platform beneath the dome, visitors could admire the lovely grounds with their neatly trimmed lawns, rose garden, orchard, croquet lawn, and tennis court. There was even an indoor swimming pool—the height of luxury. Motilal's success as a lawyer meant that he was a wealthy man, and he spared no expense. He filled Anand Bhavan with the very best that money could buy—the finest carpets, the best crystal and china, a grand piano, and even pedigree dogs. He had many items imported from London. Anand Bhavan was also the first property in Allahabad to have electricity and running water.

Kamala Nehru

"Many people know the part which was played by my grandfather and my father [in the independence movement]. But in my opinion, a more important part was played by my mother. When my father wanted to join [Mohandas Gandhi] and . . . to change our luxurious living, to give up his legal practice, the whole family was against it. It was only my mother's courageous and persistent support and encouragement which enabled him to take the big step which made such a big difference not only to our family but to the history of modern India."

(Indira, writing about her mother's
part in the Indian independence movement)

▲ *Indira's parents Jawaharlal and Kamala pose during their wedding in 1916.*

Indira later commented that the house was a delightful place in which to grow up, with plenty of space to hide and play.

The household at Anand Bhavan was a mixture of different cultures and ideas. Motilal insisted on wearing Western clothes and speaking English. His wife, Swaruprani, however, was a devout **Hindu** who wore a traditional **sari** and spoke Hindi.

Anand Bhavan's three kitchens reflected the household's different tastes. They cooked three different types of food— European, Indian vegetarian, and Indian nonvegetarian.

A lonely childhood

Despite her family's luxurious lifestyle and the number of people in the household, Indu's childhood was often lonely. Her father and grandfather were hardly ever at home, and there were no other children in the household. Her mother shared her loneliness, and the two spent a great deal of time together.

The British Raj

The Raj is the name given to the time when Great Britain governed India. The word *raj* means rule in **Hindi.** The Raj officially lasted from 1858 to 1947, although a British company, called the East India Company, controlled large parts of India before this. At the time of Indu's birth, the British **Empire** controlled India, and the British **Parliament** and Crown governed it. In London, a secretary of state for India dealt with Indian affairs in parliament. In India, an official called a **viceroy** acted as the representative of the British king or queen. At the height of the Raj, thousands of British people came to India to live and work. Most of the British considered the Indian people as inferior and kept themselves apart from them. Starting in the late 1800s, a growing group of Indians began to demand freedom from British rule. In 1885, they formed a political party called the Indian National Congress to campaign for independence. Among the Congress's leading members were Indira's grandfather Motilal and her father Jawaharlal.

▲ *King George V of England rides on an elephant (far left) during a tiger hunt in India in 1911–1912. The British controlled India from 1858 to 1947. Many members of the British Raj led rich and pampered lives.*

Gentle, frail Kamala came from a traditional **Hindu** family and was not accustomed to European ways. She did not get along with the other female members of the Nehru family, who looked down on her. They thought she was unsophisticated and not good enough for Jawaharlal. From a very young age, Indu tried to protect her mother, who was often sick. "We were very close to each other," Indira later remembered. "I loved her deeply and when I thought that she was being wronged, I fought for her and quarreled with other people." Despite her shyness and poor health, Kamala later played an important part in India's independence movement.

3 An Uncertain Childhood

To locate the places mentioned, see the map of India on page 30.

In 1919, when Indu was not even two years old, an incident occurred that changed the course of the independence struggle in India, and of Indu's childhood. On April 13, thousands of Indians gathered in a walled garden in Amritsar to protest peacefully against British rule. A British officer, General Dyer, ordered the crowd to leave the area. But his troops were blocking the only exit from the garden, and there was no way for people to get out. Dyer told his troops to wait for three minutes, then to open fire. In the **massacre** that followed, the British killed some 400 people—men, women, and children—and injured more than 1,000. Later, during an investigation of the massacre, Dyer claimed that he had not known his troops were blocking the exit. The British removed him from his post and sent him back to England.

The struggle for freedom

The Amritsar massacre was a turning point for the independence movement and for the Nehru family. Shocked and angered by the bloodshed, Indians began to realize that they would have to fight for their rights. Both Motilal and Jawaharlal pledged their full support. From then on, Anand Bhavan became a center of the independence movement. Indu got used to seeing political leaders come and go at all times of the day and night, eager to talk to her grandfather and father about the struggle for India's freedom.

Mohandas Gandhi

Among the frequent visitors to Anand Bhavan was Mohandas Gandhi, a quiet, modest lawyer, who later became the greatest leader of the struggle for Indian independence. He urged Indians not to fight the British with force, but with peaceful protest, or *satyagraha,* which means truth force.

First Jawaharlal, and later Motilal, fell under Gandhi's spell. Gandhi became a lasting inspiration throughout Indu's life. No matter how busy he was, he always had time for her. She later wrote: "He forms part of my earliest memories, and as a very small child, I regarded him not as a great leader but more as an elder of the family to whom I went with difficulties and problems which he treated with grave seriousness which was due to the large-eyed and solemn child I was." Her aunt also summed up Gandhi's effect on their lives. "He came, he saw, and he conquered. My brother has called [Gandhi's] entry into politics a gentle breeze. That makes me laugh because he came into our family like a hurricane."

Boycott bonfires

After the Amritsar massacre, Gandhi worked even harder for Indian independence. He called on Indians to **boycott** British goods, refuse to pay their taxes, and stop using British-run schools, colleges, and law courts. Like many other Indians who left well-paid jobs that required them to work with the British, Motilal and Jawaharlal gave up their legal practice to concentrate on politics. Motilal became president of the Indian National Congress, a political party that worked for independence.

At Anand Bhavan, the boycott began in earnest. One of Indu's earliest memories was of a huge bonfire upon which the family ceremonially burned their British-made clothes and other possessions, including her own favorite doll. From then on, instead of Western clothes, the Nehru family wore Indian clothes made from coarse, white **khadi** cloth. Young Indu usually dressed in a boy's khadi uniform (pants, tunic, vest, and **Gandhi cap**) of a Congress volunteer. She was often mistaken for a boy.

▲ *Followers of Gandhi burn a pile of British-made cloth in the 1920s.*

"Everybody has gone to jail"

Those were unsettling times for Indu. The British frequently
arrested her grandfather, father, aunts, and later her mother
for their part in the freedom movement. A story talks about
the day that visitors arrived at Anand Bhavan. Indu opened the
door to them and announced: "Everyone has gone to jail." In
1921, the four-year-old Indu attended her first trial. She sat on

Motilal's knee in the courtroom and listened intently. The judge sentenced Motilal and Jawaharlal to six months in jail.

For many years, Indu saw her father very little because he spent so much time in prison. The only contact she had with Jawaharlal was in the form of hundreds of letters that he wrote to her from jail. A book company later published the letters in *Glimpses From World History*. Jawaharlal meant the letters to be educational for Indu, as he taught about the whole of human history. But Jawaharlal also wrote them because he felt guilty about spending so much time away from his daughter. Indu treasured the letters.

Playing politics

Even though her family's actions often left Indu alone, she was proud of her family. She even tried to join the activities. While other children of her age played games, Indu began playing politics. She would arrange her dolls into groups of **freedom fighters** and police and act out protests. She would round up the servants at Anand Bhavan and give rousing speeches about *satyagraha*. One day, her aunt found

An insecure childhood

"As a child, when the freedom struggle was on, the house was being constantly raided by police, our goods and chattels [possessions] being confiscated. We were being arrested . . . and I was all part of it . . . It was an extremely insecure childhood. One did not know from day-to-day who would be alive, who would be in the house and what would happen next."

(Indira Gandhi in 1971, reflecting on her childhood)

her standing on the **verandah,** pretending to be Joan of Arc. She was the French heroine who rescued France from defeat in the Hundred Years' War (1337–1453) with England. Indu said that she had been reading about her. She wanted to lead India to freedom, just as Joan of Arc had done for France.

Motilal and Jawaharlal refused to pay fines demanded by the courts. So the police came to Anand Bhavan to take valuables instead. Even though she was very young, these actions made Indu furious. She shouted at the police to leave things alone and once nearly cut off an officer's thumb with a bread slicer.

Be brave

"You remember how fascinated you were when you first read the story of Jeanne d'Arc [Joan of Arc] and how your ambition was to do something like her? One little test I shall ask you to apply whenever you are in doubt. Never do anything in secret or anything you wish to hide. For, the desire that you want to hide anything means that you are afraid, and fear is a bad thing and unworthy of you. Be brave, and all the rest follows."

(Jawaharlal Nehru, in a letter written to Indira from jail)

4 Growing Up

When Indira was seven years old, her grandfather sent her to St. Cecilia's School in Allahabad. This decision infuriated her father because three British women ran the school. Jawaharlal argued that this went against the family's British **boycott.** So, he pulled Indu out of the school, and Indian tutors taught her at home.

▼ *Indira (left), at the age of about twelve, sits with her father.*

Indu's father's jail terms and her mother's poor health meant that she never attended one school for long. But she did not seem to mind. She felt out of place at St. Cecilia's because she was shy and skinny and the only girl who wore **khadi** clothes. Besides, she learned more at home sitting in the trees in the Anand Bhavan garden, reading books from her grandfather's library and listening in on conversations.

Toward the end of 1925, Indu's mother Kamala became very sick with **tuberculosis.** Her doctors advised her to go to Switzerland for treatment. In March 1926, Indu and her parents sailed from Bombay for Europe. They were away for almost two years. In Switzerland, Indu attended the International School in Geneva. The school, housed in a Swiss chalet, overlooked the stunning Alps mountain range. There, Indu studied French, music, and skiing. Later, when doctors moved Kamala to a **sanatorium** high up in the Alps, Jawaharlal enrolled Indu at a school in Bex, a town closer to her parents. This was a magical time for Indu. She traveled with her parents to Venice, Paris, London, and Berlin. The wealthy cities of Europe compared to India amazed her. But best of all she had both her parents with her—for one of the few times in her life.

TO LOCATE THE PLACES MENTIONED, SEE THE MAP OF INDIA ON PAGE 30.

The Monkey Army

By the end of 1927, Kamala had recovered enough to return to India. In 1929, Jawaharlal succeeded Motilal as the Indian National Congress president. Indu accompanied her father to the Congress meeting in Lahore where they officially proclaimed him president. Back home, she proudly watched him draft a document that set out the Congress's promise to work for full independence from Britain. When Jawaharlal had finished it, he gave it to Indu to read aloud.

Indu longed to take part in the independence movement. But at twelve years old, she was too young to join the Congress. Instead, she formed her own organization for children, called the Monkey Army. She named it after the army of monkeys in the **Hindu** sacred text the *Ramayana*, which helped the god Rama rescue his wife from a demon king. Several thousand children joined. They ran errands for the adult **Congress Party** volunteers, handed out leaflets, put up posters, and carried secret messages. The police were too busy arresting the adults to take any notice of a bunch of children!

Travels and tragedy

In February 1931, tragedy struck. After a short illness, Motilal Nehru died. Indira was heartbroken. Her grandfather had been one of the most important people in her life. She missed him terribly. Afterwards, her parents sent her to school in Poona, but she was not happy there. With her grandfather gone, her father in prison, and her mother often sick, Indu felt more homesick and lonely than ever.

Monkey business

"In their own way, the children also acted as an intelligence group [spies], because frequently the policemen sitting in front of the police station would talk about what was going on, who was to be arrested, where there would be a raid, and so on. And four or five children playing hopscotch outside would attract no one's attention. And they would deliver this news to the people in the movement."

(Indira, talking about the Monkey Army)

▲ *The great Indian poet, philosopher, and writer Rabindranath Tagore founded the university at Santiniketan, where Indira studied.*

Indu left school in 1934 and enrolled as a student at Santiniketan, the Abode of Peace. It is the school and university in Bengal founded by the great Indian poet and philosopher Rabindranath Tagore. She loved the peace and quiet of Santiniketan, and Tagore awed her. She quickly adapted to the tough living conditions, sleeping on a mat on the floor and taking cold baths. Classes began at 7:00 A.M. Indu's favorite class was Indian dance, and she became an accomplished performer in just a few months. But her happiness did not last long. As Indu was rehearsing for a

TO LOCATE THE PLACES MENTIONED, SEE THE MAP OF INDIA ON PAGE 30.

dance performance, a telegram arrived. Her mother's health had broken down again, and she had to leave for Europe as soon as possible. With a heavy heart, Indu packed her bags and said her good-byes.

Indu and Kamala arrived in Europe in June 1935, then traveled to a **sanatorium** in southern Germany. The sanatorium depressed Indu, and she became worn out by the strain of looking after her mother. But Kamala's health got worse, and she asked to be moved to Lausanne, Switzerland. She died there on February 28, 1936. She was only 36 years old. Jawaharlal, who had been released from prison to be with his wife, was with Indu at Kamala's bedside. Kamala's death devastated Indu. She felt more alone than ever. For years, she and Kamala had taken care of each other. Whom could she turn to now?

Rare qualities

"Kamala possessed qualities rarely found in other women. I am hoping that all these qualities of Kamala will be manifest in you in equal measure. May God give you long life and strength to emulate her virtues."

(Mohandas Gandhi in a letter to Indira on the death of her mother)

England

After Kamala's death, Indu went to school and college in England. In October 1936, she started at Badminton School in preparation for the Oxford University entrance exam. The headmistress of the school was a great admirer of Indira's father. A fellow pupil remembers that Indu looked frail and unhappy and could not wait to go back home to India. Indu herself complained to her father that she found the school rules stifling.

A year later, Indu went to Somerville College in Oxford, England, to study history. She fit in well, although she did not like her classes. In Oxford and London, she got to know many Indian students who were eager to meet Nehru's daughter. Among them was Feroze Gandhi (no relation to Mohandas Gandhi). Feroze was a family friend who was active in the Congress and had been devoted to Kamala. In England, his friendship with Indu quickly blossomed into love.

▼ Jawaharlal (right) accompanied Indu (left) on the trip to Oxford, England, where she would attend school.

5 Marriage

In 1941, as World War II engulfed Europe, Indira and Feroze decided to leave London and return to India. They caught a ship to Bombay that stopped at the Cape of Good Hope at the southern tip of Africa. There, they visited Durban, South Africa, where the city's large Indian community warmly welcomed Indira. They asked Indira to speak at a reception in her honor. She agreed, but reluctantly—she was not used to speaking in public.

Driving around Durban, the desperate conditions in which black people lived under the country's racist regime appalled her. That evening, so angered by what she saw that day, Indira forgot her nervousness for public speaking. She lectured her Indian audience on the evils of the regime and criticized them for not doing more to help black people fight against it. Her speech did not go over well.

Marriage

Back home, Indira told her father that she intended to marry Feroze as soon as possible. Indira's decision did not please Nehru. He told her not to rush into anything. In fact, he did not think Feroze was good enough for her. For one thing, Feroze came from a poor family. He did not share Indira's wealthy background. But when it became clear that Indira had made up her mind, Nehru asked her to consult Mohandas Gandhi. If Gandhi agreed to the match, Nehru would not object. After seeing both Indira and Feroze, Gandhi gave his blessing. Not everyone was in favor, though. News of Indira's engagement filled the newspapers, and many people became hostile. Nehru allowing his daughter, a **Hindu,** to marry Feroze, a **Parsi,** outraged many people. In India, at that time, most people married someone who belonged to the same religion as they did.

▲ *Indira (right) and Feroze Gandhi (left) celebrate their wedding day on March 26, 1942.*

The wedding of Indira and Feroze took place on March 26, 1942, on the grounds of Anand Bhavan. Indira dressed simply in a **khadi sari** woven by her father during one of his stays in prison. Feroze wore the khadi dress of the **Congress Party.** The ceremony was traditionally **Hindu.** Indira and Feroze took seven steps around the sacred fire and vowed to love and care for each other for the rest of their lives. But Indira also made another vow—to fight against those who tried to prevent her country from achieving its freedom.

To LOCATE THE PLACES MENTIONED, SEE THE MAP OF INDIA ON PAGE 30.

Quit India

After their wedding, Indira and Feroze left for a two-month honeymoon in Kashmir. It was a magical time for them both. "Truly if there is a heaven," Indira wrote, "it must be this. . . ."

But no sooner were they back home, than they were thrown
into political life once more. World War II was well underway,
and millions of Indians fought for Britain. In return, Britain
promised to grant India independence. So far, Britain had not
kept these promises. In August 1942, Mohandas Gandhi
launched the Quit India movement. If the British did not leave
India at once, the protests, strikes, **boycotts,** and other acts
of disobedience would start up again. In an effort to control
the situation, the British arrested Congress Party leaders,
including Gandhi and Nehru. The British imprisoned
thousands of protesters without trial. But that act did not
stop the unrest that swept through India.

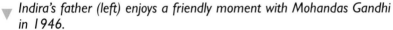

Indira's father (left) enjoys a friendly moment with Mohandas Gandhi in 1946.

Prison

Indira and Feroze threw themselves into the Quit India campaign. In September 1942, Indira spoke at a public meeting, even though the British government had banned such gatherings. They arrested her and Feroze. They took Indira to Naini Jail in Allahabad, where they had often held her father. Indira did not find prison life easy. "The ground, the walls, everything around us is mud-colored," Indira wrote, "and so became our jailwashed clothes." She kept her spirits up, even though the British considered her so dangerous that they did not allow her any visitors. To pass the time, she read, wrote in her diary, and taught other prisoners. She also helped to care for another prisoner's baby. Indira expected a long sentence, but the British released her in May 1943, after eight months.

Two months later, they also freed Feroze, and he and Indira went to stay at Anand Bhavan. On August 20, 1944, their first child, a boy they named Rajiv, was born. Feroze hoped that now that Indira had a baby to care for she would spend more time at home. But even though Indira was devoted to her son, she was too involved in her political work to become a stay-at-home mother.

On motherhood

"To bring a new being into this world, to see its tiny perfection and to dream of its future greatness is the most moving of all experiences and fills one with wonder and **exaltation.**"

(Indira, on becoming a mother)

6 Freedom at Midnight

By the time World War II ended in August 1945, Britain could not stop the **nationalist** unrest in India. The British knew they could not rule India for much longer. They began to take steps to hand over power. The British released Indira's father, along with the other **Congress Party** leaders, from prison to take part in talks with the British government. In September 1946, Nehru was asked to head an **interim government** that would lead India to independence. In effect, he was now **prime minister** of India.

Official duties

This was an exciting time for Indira. But life was also hectic. Located in Lucknow, the *National Herald,* a Congress Party newspaper, appointed Feroze as its new managing director. He and Indira moved to a rented bungalow in Lucknow. But their settled life did not last for long. With his new responsibilities, Nehru's life was now busier than ever. A constant stream of visitors demanded his time, and Indira felt that it was her duty to support and help him. Not for the first time in her life, Indira was torn between her husband and her father. She began to divide her time between Delhi, where Nehru lived, and Lucknow. But it was a night's journey by train between the two cities, and the traveling left Indira exhausted.

To LOCATE THE PLACES MENTIONED, SEE THE MAP OF INDIA ON PAGE 30.

On December 14, 1946, Indira and Feroze's second son, Sanjay, was born. Indira was thrilled. She doted on her sons. Despite her busy schedule, she tried to make as much time as possible for them. One day, a woman remarked that Indira could not have much time left over from her work to spend with her sons. Sanjay rushed to her rescue with the words: "My mother does lots of important work, yet she plays with me more than you do with your little boy."

Independence

At the stroke of midnight on August 15, 1947, India became an independent country. Indira was present in the Indian **parliament** when her father made his historic speech:

> Long years ago we made a tryst [secret date] with destiny and now the time comes when we shall redeem our pledge, not wholly or in full measure but very substantially. At the stroke of the midnight hour when the world sleeps, India will awake to life and freedom.

The next day, Nehru was sworn in as the first **prime minister** of India, and he ceremonially raised the **saffron**-white-and-green Indian flag. History was being made. It was a moment that the 29-year-old Indira would never forget. At last it seemed that everything she and her family had struggled for was happening.

▼ *Lord Mountbatten, the British **viceroy**, announces Indian independence in 1947.*

▲ *Jubilant crowds in Bombay celebrate India's independence in August 1947.*

But there was a price to pay for freedom. India's **Hindus** and **Muslims** were united in their wish for the British to leave. But they disagreed violently about the future of India. The Muslims thought that an India led by **Hindus** would be as bad for them as one led by the British. For many years, the All-India Muslim League had been campaigning for a separate country for the millions of Indian Muslims. They wanted a new country called Pakistan, and it would include parts of the states of Punjab in the west and Bengal in the east. The two sides agreed that India should be partitioned and, on August 14, 1947, Pakistan came into being. They divided it into two parts—West Pakistan and East Pakistan—separated by Indian territory.

TO LOCATE THE PLACES MENTIONED, SEE THE MAP OF INDIA ON PAGE 30.

On independence

"It was impossible to take in that after all these years something we had thought of and dreamt of and worked for ever since I could remember, had happened. It was such a powerful experience that I think I was numb. You know when you go to an extreme of pleasure or pain, there is numbness. Freedom was just so big a thing that it could not register. It seemed to fill all of you and all your world."

(Indira talking about India's independence)

29

Terrible violence and bloodshed marked the partition of India. Many **Muslims** who found themselves living in the new India fled to Pakistan. And **Hindus** in the new Pakistan fled to India. Families packed up their belongings, left their homes, and desperately tried to escape over the new borders. In the chaos, violence between Hindus and Muslims killed hundreds of thousands of people. Many of these people, who had previously lived together in peace, now turned on each other. **Refugees** began pouring into India from Pakistan.

In Delhi, Mohandas Gandhi urged Indira to help in the refugee camps where thousands of starving, thirsty people lived in filthy conditions. Cholera, typhoid, and other life-threatening

▼ *This map shows India's national borders after its partition.*

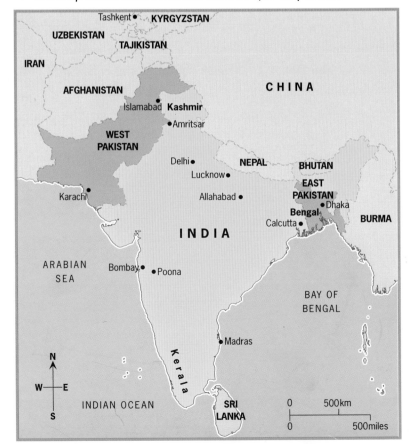

diseases spread through the camps. Soon, Indira was spending up to twelve hours a day in the camps, passing out food, water, and medical supplies and trying to reassure the terrified refugees. It was difficult and dangerous work because of the threat of disease and violence. But she was determined to do what she could. Besides, as she once told her father, she coped best in a crisis.

▶ *Muslim refugees from India crowd onto a train bound for Pakistan.*

Key dates: Toward independence

1858	India comes under British rule
1885	The Indian National Congress is founded
1906	The All-India Muslim League is formed
1920	Mohandas Gandhi launches his noncooperation campaign
1935	The Government of India Act gives Indians a greater say in the government of the country
1942	Gandhi launches the Quit India movement to force the British to leave India
1947	India and Pakistan become independent

For the next seventeen years, Indira acted as her father's official hostess, running his household and accompanying him on foreign trips. She moved to Delhi to be with him, taking Rajiv and Sanjay with her. The **prime minister**'s official residence in Delhi was a magnificent house called Teen Murti House, or the House of the Three Statues. It was named after the statues of three soldiers that stand at its entrance. In the days of the Raj, Teen Murti had belonged to the British commander-in-chief.

Keeping house

Keeping house for Nehru was a daunting task. Teen Murti was a huge house, with long corridors and enormous rooms, including a ballroom and a banquet hall. Indira did her best to make it feel like home. She replaced the dark oil paintings with Indian artwork and had the walls painted white. She was responsible for the whole household. This meant taking care of the huge number of guests, planning

▲ *Indira (right) with her father and her oldest son Rajiv in 1950 on the grounds of Teen Murti.*

menus and seating for dinners, supervising the servants and staff, and caring for her father and sons. Many of the guests followed special diets, and one of her most difficult jobs was making sure that they all got the right thing to eat.

Traveling companion

Indira often traveled with her father. In October 1949, she went with him to the United States on her first official trip abroad. In New York City, she went to art galleries, to the theater, and to fashionable restaurants. She also met many important U.S. politicians. Later, she accompanied Nehru to countries throughout the world. It was the best training in politics anyone could have.

In April 1953, Indira, Rajiv, and Sanjay sailed to England to attend the **coronation** of Queen Elizabeth II. Nehru joined them later. After the celebrations, Indira traveled to the Soviet Union for the first time. It was her first trip on her own as the prime minister's daughter. She liked the country very much, and the Soviet people welcomed her warmly in return.

Indian government

India is a **republic** with a parliamentary system of government. There are two houses of **parliament**—the Lok Sabha (House of the People) and the Rajya Sabha (Council of States)—to which the members of parliament (MPs) belong. The president is the head of state, and the prime minister is the head of the government. Each of India's 26 states also has its own chief ministers and **legislative assemblies,** which answer to the central government. All Indians over the age of eighteen can vote in the general elections. These are usually held every five years.

India held its first general election in 1951–1952. Many people urged Indira to run for **parliament,** but she refused. She did not feel that she was yet ready for political life. Instead, she worked tirelessly, traveling around the country to campaign for her father. The **Congress Party** won the election with a huge majority over the opposition parties, and voters reelected Nehru. But Nehru began to turn to Indira more and more for political advice, and he often asked her to stand in for him at political meetings.

In 1955, Congress Party members elected Indira as a member of the Working Committee of the Congress Party. It was a turning point for Indira. She had finally become a political figure in her own right. People whispered that Nehru had pulled some strings to get his daughter elected to this important party position. But according to Indira, her father's only piece of advice about her entrance into politics was for her to make her own decisions.

Indira rose quickly through the ranks of the Congress Party. On February 2, 1959, party members elected her president of the party, following in her father's and grandfather's footsteps. She served for just under a year. In her short presidential speech, she asked to be treated like any other ordinary party worker.

◀ *Indira doted on her sons, Rajiv age eight (center) and Sanjay age six (right).*

The death of Feroze

Voters, meanwhile, had elected Feroze as a member of parliament (MP). He moved to Delhi, but he did not feel welcome at Teen Murti and lived in his own government bungalow. He visited Teen Murti only to see his sons when they were home from boarding school.

▲ *Indira accompanied her father on a trip to London, England, in 1956.*

Indira and Feroze's marriage was becoming strained. Feroze felt left out of the Nehru family and resented how Indira always seemed to be at her father's beck and call.

In 1958, Feroze suffered a heart attack. For a short while, he and Indira had reconciled. On a family vacation in Kashmir, they even spoke of building their own house on a lot that Feroze had bought. But in September 1960, Feroze suffered another serious heart attack. Indira flew back from Kerala, where she had been speaking at a conference. She went straight to Feroze's bedside at the hospital and sat there all night, holding his hand. He died early the next morning, at the age of 48.

On the campaign trail

"One of the surprises of this election . . . has been the very fine work done by Indira. She has worked terribly hard. In Delhi, she used to go out at eight in the morning and return about eleven at night addressing numerous small meetings and groups. She is reported to be a very effective speaker and is in great demand."

(Nehru describing how hard Indira campaigned for him during the 1951–1952 general election)

*Party members elected Indira as president of the **Congress Party** in 1959.*

Feroze's death shattered Indira. She had not expected to lose her husband so young. For the first few days, she felt numb. Then, when her sons returned to boarding school, she wrote in a letter to Rajiv: "But now I have begun to cry and do not seem to be able to stop. I have never before known such desolation and grief."

Losing her father

After Feroze died, Indira threw herself into politics again. She traveled to Mexico, the United States, and Britain. Back in India, trouble was brewing. In October 1962, China invaded northern India. It took the Indian government by surprise and, as a result, the army was totally unprepared. Indira flew to the front line, taking **Red Cross** supplies. The Chinese invasion

On Feroze's death

"I was actually physically ill. It upset my whole being for years, which is strange, because after all he was very, very ill, and I should have expected that he would die. However, it was not just a mental pain, but it was as though somebody had cut me in two."

(Indira, remembering Feroze's death)

ended as quickly as it had begun, just a few weeks later. But the short invasion had done the damage. Indians held Nehru responsible for the military disaster, and his popularity dipped. Some people thought that, at the age of 72, he was too old to be **prime minister.** His health began to break down and, in January 1964, he suffered a stroke. The stroke left Nehru partially paralyzed and confined to a wheelchair. Indira devoted all her energy to caring for him. Then, on the morning of May 27, Nehru suffered another stroke. He died at 1:44 P.M., without regaining consciousness.

Grief overcame Indira. But she was not alone. Millions of Indians shared her feelings. More than two million mourners lined the funeral route to pay their last respects. One of the most touching notes of sympathy came from a child who wrote to Indira: "I like your father very much . . . Do not cry or I will also cry." Later, Indira scattered her father's ashes in the sacred river at Allahabad and in Kashmir. Afterwards, she sank into a deep depression. With her husband and father gone and her sons growing up (Rajiv was twenty years old and Sanjay eighteen years old), Indira felt a deep sense of loss.

▶ *The body of Jawaharlal Nehru lays in state in May 1964. (Indira is on the far left of this picture.)*

Prime Minister Gandhi

With Nehru gone, the competition to succeed him began in earnest. Backed by the most powerful members of the **Congress Party,** called the Syndicate, Lal Bahadur Shastri, a quiet, modest man, was appointed **prime minister.** Indira moved out of Teen Murti House and into a spacious government bungalow at One Safdarjung Road. The new prime minister did not want to live in Teen Murti, and the government later turned the house into the Nehru Museum.

▲ *Lal Bahadur Shastri served as prime minister of India from 1964 to 1966.*

Shastri invited Indira to become minister of information and broadcasting in his **cabinet.** It was her first government post. In order to become a cabinet minister, Indira had first to become an MP. The Congress Party appointed her to the Rajya Sabha, the upper house of the Indian **parliament.** Indira worked hard at her new job. She weakened laws that **censored** movies, extended broadcasting hours, and supported the use of television and radio in education.

But Shastri also recognized Indira's usefulness as an ambassador for India. She was elegant and charming and could speak fluent English and French. He sent her on several trips abroad on the government's behalf.

Prime minister

In January 1966, Shastri flew to Tashkent, the capital of Uzbekistan, which was then part of the Soviet Union. There, he met with Pakistan's leader to try to settle the dispute over Kashmir. Afterwards, he complained of feeling tired and went to his room. He died later that night of a massive heart attack. When the shocking news reached India, his death threw the government into turmoil once again.

To locate the places mentioned, see the map of India on page 30.

This time the Syndicate backed Indira for prime minister. They thought that she would do what they told her to do because of her lack of experience in government. She would also prove a certain vote winner in the next general election, thanks to the magic of the Gandhi and Nehru names. In the Congress Party election, Indira defeated her closest rival, Morarji Desai, by 186 votes and became India's first woman **prime minister.** But the Syndicate had underestimated her. Indira was nobody's puppet. She may have lacked experience, but a sharp mind and enormous courage and determination lurked beneath her quiet exterior. She also firmly believed that she was the only person who could lead India.

Indira soon put her political skills to the test. India had suffered a terrible **drought,** and many states were facing **famine.** In some places the rice harvest had failed for two years, leading to unrest and rioting. The country desperately needed foreign aid. In March 1966, Indira visited the United States for talks with President Lyndon Johnson.

▲ *Prime Minister Indira Gandhi (center) visited President Lyndon Johnson and his wife Lady Bird in the United States in 1966.*

President Johnson promised to give India 3 million tons of food and $9 million in aid. In return, he wanted India to be less critical of U.S. involvement in the **Vietnam War.** Indira agreed, but back in India the **Congress Party** criticized the deal. Indira argued that she was doing what she had to do for the good of the country.

At the same time, Indira established closer relations with the Soviet Union. At that time, the United States and the Soviet Union were enemies. Indira thought India would benefit from being allied with the Soviet Union. The two countries issued a joint statement denouncing the U.S. bombing of Vietnam. This announcement infuriated the United States, and they withdrew their promise of aid. With the general election only months away, Indira found herself with enemies at home and abroad.

Indira's qualities

"She knows all the world leaders, has traveled widely with her father, has grown up amongst the great men of the freedom movement, has a rational and modern mind, is totally free of any **parochialism**—state, **caste,** or religion. She has probably inherited her father's scientific temper [logical, ordered mind] and, above all, she can win the election of 1967."

(K. Kamaraj, a leading Indian politician, on the decision to back Indira for prime minister)

Second term

Indira traveled throughout India campaigning for votes to try to win the 1967 general election. She spoke at hundreds of meetings and drew huge crowds. Indira always thought it was important to keep in touch with the ordinary people of India. This time she wanted the Indian people—not just her party—to elect her to the post of **prime minister.** In her campaign speeches, she spoke in simple language so that ordinary people could understand. They were her family, she said, and she would take care of them. In return, the people gave her a new title—"Mother Indira."

▶ A poster encourages Indians to vote for Indira Gandhi and the Congress Party in the 1967 general election.

The **Congress Party** won the 1967 general election. Indira was more popular than ever and won her seat with an increased majority. She was reelected party leader and **prime minister.** In a clever move, she appointed her main rival, Morarji Desai, to the important post of deputy prime minister.

The party splits

But deep divisions existed within the Congress Party between Indira's supporters and enemies. Matters came to a head in May 1969, when the president of India died suddenly. Indira's choice of candidate to succeed him was the vice-president V. V. Giri. But her enemies in the Congress Party did not agree. They wanted to nominate one of their own members, Sanjiva Reddy. Indira decided that the time had come to get tough and do things her way. First, she pushed through plans to **nationalize** India's banks. This move was popular with ordinary people but not with the Congress Party. Next, she announced that Giri would run against Reddy. It was a huge risk, but it paid off when voters elected Giri. The election infuriated many Congress Party leaders, and they accused Indira of acting against the interests of the party.

In November 1969, the Congress Party split into two factions—Congress (O) and Congress (R). Congress (O), or Old Congress, was the old guard, led by Morarji Desai. Indira led Congress (R), or Ruling Congress. But Indira's position was still uncertain. With Congress (O) determined to get rid of her once and for all, Indira made her surprise move. She called a general election for March 1971, a year earlier than required by law. She would ask the Indian people to decide her future.

Indira campaigned tirelessly for the 1971 election, touring the country and addressing millions of people. With her campaign slogan of "Garibi Hatao," or "Remove Poverty," she pledged to do more to help India's poor. It proved to be a vote winner. When authorities declared the results of the election, Indira's Congress (R) had won a landslide victory. Indira was back in power and more popular than ever.

Bangladesh

Since Pakistan's creation in 1947, a conflict existed between the two parts of the country. East and West Pakistan stood more than 900 miles (1,450 kilometers) apart, on opposite sides of India. They did not even share a common language— West Pakistanis spoke Urdu, and East Pakistanis spoke Bengali. West Pakistan, under a **military dictatorship,** was larger and wealthier. It dominated the poorer East Pakistan. The East Pakistanis began to demand their freedom.

▼ *Indira is sworn in as prime minister in 1971.*

TO LOCATE THE PLACES MENTIONED, SEE THE MAP OF INDIA ON PAGE 30.

In 1971, **civil war** broke out between East and West Pakistan. West Pakistan sent troops into Dhaka, the East Pakistani capital, to restore law and order. India backed East Pakistan and accepted the millions of **refugees** who began to pour across the border. In December, West Pakistan declared war on India, and its air force bombed nine Indian air bases. But Indira was ready. She immediately sent Indian troops to East Pakistan to put down the West Pakistani forces and support the **freedom fighters.** On December 16, 1971, the West Pakistani army surrendered, and East Pakistan became the independent country of Bangladesh.

Free Bangladesh

"I have an announcement to make, which I think the House has been waiting for, for some time. The West Pakistan forces have unconditionally surrendered in Bangladesh . . . Dhaka is now the free capital of a free country. This House and the entire nation rejoice in this historic event. We hail the people of Bangladesh in their hour of triumph."

(Indira speaking to the Indian parliament on the surrender of the Pakistani army on December 16, 1971)

It was Indira's finest hour. In both India and Bangladesh, people hailed her as a heroine for winning the war and helping to free a nation. She had shown that she could be a tough, shrewd, and strong leader. Indeed, many people were calling her the greatest leader India had ever had.

Work and family

As **prime minister,** Indira's day began early, at about 6:00 A.M. First, she did yoga exercises for about twenty minutes. She then ate breakfast on a tray in her bedroom and

▲ *Indira shakes hands with Sheikh Mujibur Rahman, the first **prime minister** of Bangladesh, in 1972.*

read the newspapers. Then she met with her private secretary to go over the day's schedule. Afterwards, Indira held her morning *darshan* (public audience) in the garden of One Akbar Road. This was the bungalow next door to her own house where she had her offices. For an hour, people from all walks of life could come to meet the prime minister and tell her about their problems. By 10:00 A.M., Indira was usually at her desk. She went home to One Safdarjung Road for lunch at 1:00 P.M., then returned to her office to work until 7:00 or 8:00 P.M. After dinner with the family, she worked until midnight or entertained visitors. She rarely managed to get more than five or six hours of sleep a night.

By now, Indira was sharing her home at One Safdarjung Road with her older son Rajiv and his Italian wife Sonia. Sonia and Indira got along very well, and Indira doted on her two grandchildren, Rahul and Priyanka, who often slept in her room at night. Sonia quickly adapted to Indian life and ran the Gandhi household. After their marriage in 1974, Sanjay, Indira's younger son, and his wife Maneka also lived in Indira's home.

New challenges

In 1972, Indira faced a new challenge. The country suffered a terrible **drought** when the **monsoon** rains failed. The drought caused a poor harvest, and serious food shortages resulted. At the same time, the economy was getting worse. Prices rose sharply, and **corruption** grew. India was in a state of turmoil, with widespread food riots, strikes, and **industrial unrest.** In 1973–1974, the monsoon rains failed again. What had happened to Indira's election promises? The poor were now worse off than ever. Indira's campaign slogan came back to haunt her. In place of "Remove Poverty," her opponents chanted "Remove Indira" instead.

▼ Indira declares the state of emergency in 1975 in Delhi.

Then came another blow. In 1975, India's high court found Indira guilty of corruption during the 1971 election campaign. Her opponents demanded that she resign, but Indira refused. She felt it was her duty to stay and lead her country. On June 26, 1975, she declared a state of emergency, claiming that forces inside and out were threatening India's security. The court overturned her conviction, but the state of emergency remained.

Ruthless streak

The state of emergency showed Indira's **ruthless** streak. It involved the arrest of thousands of opposition leaders and demonstrators. She harshly **censored** the press, and she declared strikes, **sit-ins,** and demonstrations illegal and quickly crushed them. At first, many of these measures proved popular because they restored order to India's riot-torn cities. But Indira often acted on her own, without first getting the approval of **parliament.** Her opponents accused her of being a **dictator** and of working to destroy India's **democracy.**

And the situation got even worse. During the state of emergency, Indira began to rely more and more on the advice of her younger son Sanjay. Her actions had left her on bad terms with her colleagues, and she needed someone she could trust. Indira made no secret that she was grooming Sanjay to succeed her. But Sanjay was no Indira or Nehru. Many people thought that he was irresponsible, a person who preferred driving fast cars and flying planes to hard work. Sanjay's increasing hold over his mother worried them. But few dared speak out openly against the **prime minister's** son. And even if Indira was aware of her son's behavior, she turned a blind eye.

▲ *Indira (right) relied more and more on her son, Sanjay (left), as conditions in the country grew more troublesome.*

It was Sanjay who introduced the two most disastrous policies of the state of emergency—family planning and slum clearance. India's population was growing fast, by about twelve million people a year. Everyone agreed that for the lives of the poor to improve, population growth had to slow down. The government also needed to do something to provide them with better housing.

But Sanjay put his policies into practice in a way that created great suffering among the poor—the very people Indira had claimed the state of emergency would help. The government rounded up terrified villagers and forced them to have an operation to **sterilize** them. In return, the government gave them money, a can of cooking oil, or a radio. The government also cleared city slums without any thought of where the people who lived there would go. In Delhi, a large, rambling area of run-down houses and shacks had grown up around the Jama Masjid, the city's old main **mosque.** People had lived there for centuries. But Sanjay **ruthlessly** ordered the buildings to be demolished for the sake of the beautification of Delhi. He gave families and store owners only an hour or so to clear out before the bulldozers arrived. When people protested, the police opened fire on them.

The aftermath

Sanjay's actions shocked and angered even Indira's closest allies. Criticized at home and abroad, Indira could no longer ignore what was happening. The state of emergency and Sanjay were spiralling out of control and harming Indira's reputation. Instead of getting rid of poverty, her opponents said, Indira was getting rid of the poor. Indira's love of Sanjay had blinded her to his faults. She had now lost the respect of those that mattered most to her—the ordinary people of India. In January 1977, Indira relaxed the state of emergency, released the political leaders, and called a general election for March. But the people voted against her. The Janata Party defeated the Congress Party, and Indira lost her seat. Her bitter enemy, Morarji Desai, was sworn in as leader of the newly formed Janata Party and became **prime minister.**

▼ *Opposition leader Morarji Desai addresses a rally as campaigning began for the 1977 general election.*

10 Troubled Final Years

For the first time in her life, Indira had become a political outsider. She also found herself homeless. She left One Safdarjung Road and moved into the house of an old family friend. But she was determined to fight back. In May 1977, she formed her own new party called Congress I (for Indira). In the state elections of February 1978, the party fielded several candidates, including Indira. She won a seat in Karnataka in southern India and was reelected to **parliament** as an MP.

◁ *Indira campaigns during the 1978 state elections.*

Return to power

By 1980, the ruling Janata Party led by Morarji Desai was in disorder. It had no real policies and failed to keep its promises of helping India's poor. Once again, the country fell into chaos with rising prices, a rising crime rate, and a weak economy. In 1979, Desai resigned as **prime minister,** and Charan Singh succeeded him. He dissolved parliament and called a general election for January 1980.

TO LOCATE THE PLACES MENTIONED, SEE THE MAP OF INDIA ON PAGE 30.

Meanwhile, Indira was hard at work saving her reputation. She traveled all over India and received a warm welcome wherever she went. With the Janata Party in shambles, many people felt that Indira was the only person who really understood India. In the elections, Congress I won with a large majority. At 62 years old, Indira became prime minister

▶ *Indira waves to the crowds as she tours India to win support for her Congress I party.*

for a fourth term. It was a great comeback. Sanjay also won his seat and continued to be his mother's closest adviser. But Indira did not give him a post in her new **cabinet.** Perhaps she realized what people would say. Instead, she appointed him general secretary of the party, a post she herself had held.

But the joy of her victory was short-lived. On June 23, 1980, Sanjay died in a plane crash. He was 33 years old. His death stunned Indira. Friends said that she never really recovered from this tragedy. Sanjay had been her favorite son and most trusted adviser. She had depended on him utterly. Desperate to keep the family tradition going, she persuaded Rajiv to resign his job as an airline pilot and join the **Congress Party.** In 1981, voters elected Rajiv to his brother's vacant seat in parliament.

Key dates: Indira's terms of office

1966–1967	First term
1967–1971	Second term
1971–1977	Third term
1980–1984	Fourth term

▲ *Indira listens to a Sikh man's complaints during her daily* darshan *(audience) a few weeks before her death.*

Operation Blue Star

Over the next few years, Indira faced new calls for independence from several Indian states that did not feel that the central government was meeting their needs. In Punjab, trouble was brewing as a group of **militant Sikhs,** led by Jarnail Singh Bhindranwale, demanded a separate Sikh state. The Sikh religion had been founded in Punjab in the 1500s, and its millions of followers still lived mostly in the state. Bhindranwale and his heavily armed followers occupied the Golden Temple in Amritsar, the Sikhs' most sacred shrine. From there, they waged a war of violence and **terrorism** against the government. When negotiations broke down, Indira knew that she needed to take drastic action.

On June 6, 1984, Indira sent the Indian army into the Golden Temple to remove Bhindranwale and his men. Operation Blue Star, the campaign's official government name, had begun. In the fighting that followed, up to 1,000 Sikhs, including Bhindranwale, and 300 soldiers were killed. The operation badly damaged the Golden Temple and riddled the Akal Takht, its most sacred shrine, with bullet holes. The Sikhs swore to get their revenge for the devastation of their holiest place.

Assassination

After Operation Blue Star, Indira knew that Sikhs wanted revenge and that her life was in danger. On the morning of October 31, 1984, she left home to go to her office, a few minutes walk away, for a television interview. Since Operation

Addressing the nation

"Indira Gandhi has been assassinated. She was mother not only to me but to the whole nation. She served the Indian people to her last drop of blood . . . We can and must face this tragic ordeal with **fortitude,** courage, and wisdom."

(Rajiv Gandhi in a speech following his mother's death, 1984)

Blue Star, she had started wearing a bullet-proof vest, but she had not put it on today. As she reached the garden gate, she turned to greet her Sikh bodyguards— Beant Singh, who had worked for her for many years, and a younger man, Satwant Singh. Without warning, Beant Singh pulled out his revolver. He shot her at point-blank range. Satwant Singh also opened fire. Indira fell to the ground. In the chaos that followed, authorities arrested Beant Singh and Satwant Singh, and an ambulance rushed Indira to the hospital. At 2:23 P.M., doctors pronounced Indira Gandhi dead.

On the evening of his mother's death, the **Congress Party** swore Rajiv in as president and **prime minister** of India. One of his first acts was to try to stop the rioting sparked off by Indira's death. In Delhi and other Indian cities, violence killed some 2,500 people, as angry **Hindus** attacked Sikhs. Because of the unrest, few people lined the Delhi streets to witness Indira's funeral procession on its way to the cremation

grounds on the banks of the Jumna River in Delhi. It was a sad end to an extraordinary life.

◀ *Indira's funeral procession makes its way through the streets of Delhi.*

53

11 Impact and Legacy

As the first woman **prime minister** of India, a society in which men traditionally held most, or all, of the power, Indira Gandhi earned her place in history. But opinion is divided about her lasting legacy. Loved and hated equally, Indira was both a strong and **ruthless** political leader but also a warm, loving mother and doting grandmother.

During her lifetime

As prime minister, Indira had many achievements to her name. She was the leader of the world's largest **democracy.** Despite the country's huge size and frequent outbreaks of religious violence, Indira managed to keep it largely united. Her regular trips abroad strengthened the relationships with foreign powers that her father had begun and helped get India noticed by other countries. But her poor handling of the state of emergency earned her many lasting enemies who accused her of ruling as a **dictator.** In her personal life, her failure to control Sanjay harmed her greatly. People criticized her for trying to build a ruling **dynasty** rather than a democracy. In later years, her determination to rule India from the center caused great resentment among the states. This resentment led to her death.

◀ *The Indira Gandhi memorial sits in a lush tree-filled setting in Delhi.*

Thoughts of death

"If I die a violent death, as some fear and a few are plotting, I know the violence will be in the thought and action of the assassin, not in my dying—for no hate is dark enough to overshadow the extent of my love for my people and my country. No force is strong enough to divert me from my purpose and my endeavor to take this country forward."

(Indira in 1984)

◀ *Indira speaks in Jaipur in 1984, shortly before her death. Her legacy remains as one of India's most remarkable leaders.*

After her death

Since her death, people continue to feel Indira's influence across India. Thousands of places are named after her—airports, hospitals, museums, schools, and colleges. But today, the **Congress Party,** which she led for so long, has little power. The party lost the 1989 elections, and her son Rajiv, her successor, was assassinated in 1991 while campaigning. In early 2000, his wife Sonia Gandhi became president of the Congress Party and leader of the opposition in the Indian **parliament.**

Despite the highs and lows that marked her personal and political life, no doubt exists that Indira Gandhi was a remarkable leader. She genuinely loved India and believed that she was doing her best for her country. In her last speech, made the day before she died, Indira said: "I shall continue to serve until my last breath and, when I die, I can say that every drop of my blood will **invigorate** India and strengthen it."

Timeline

1917	Born Indira Priyadarshini Nehru in Allahabad, India, on November 19
1919	Amritsar massacre
1920	Mohandas Gandhi launches campaign of nonviolent disobedience (*satyagraha*) to protest British rule
1926	Sails to Europe with her parents Attends school in Switzerland
1929	Forms Monkey Army
1931	Motilal Nehru dies
1934	Enrolls at Santiniketan University
1935	Travels to Europe with her mother
1936	Kamala, Indira's mother, dies in Switzerland Attends Badminton School, England
1937	Begins studies at Somerville College
1939–1945	World War II
1941	Returns to India
1942	Quit India Campaign Marries Feroze Gandhi Indira and Feroze arrested and jailed
1943	Released from prison
1944	First son Rajiv born
1946	Second son Sanjay born

1947	India gains independence from Great Britain Nehru becomes prime minister India partitioned and Pakistan created
1948	Mohandas Gandhi assassinated
1955	Elected to the Working Committee of the Congress Party
1959	Elected president of the Congress Party
1960	Feroze Gandhi dies
1962	China invades northern India
1964	Nehru dies Becomes minister of information and broadcasting
1966	Sworn in as prime minister
1967	Wins second term in office
1971	**Civil war** in Pakistan East Pakistan becomes Bangladesh
1971	Wins third term in office
1975	Declares state of emergency
1977	State of emergency ended Defeated in general election Morarji Desai becomes prime minister
1980	Returns to power for fourth term Sanjay dies in a plane crash
1984	Sends troops into Golden Temple to put down Sikh militants Assassinated by her Sikh bodyguards

Key People of Gandhi's Time

Desai, Morarji (1896–1995) Desai was **prime minister** of India from 1977 to 1979. As leader of the Janata Party, he became prime minister after Indira Gandhi's defeat in the general election. An enemy of Indira's, he resigned from office in 1979.

Gandhi, Feroze (1912–1960) Gandhi was Indira's husband and father of Rajiv and Sanjay. He married Indira in 1942. He died of a heart attack in September 1960.

Gandhi, Mohandas (1869–1948) Born in Gujarat in western India, Gandhi practiced as a lawyer in England and South Africa, where he led the nonviolent struggle for the civil rights of Indian workers. Later, as leader of the movement for Indian independence, he applied the technique of *satyagraha,* or nonviolent protest, to the freedom struggle. A close friend of the Nehru family, he was assassinated in 1948 by a Hindu extremist. He was known as *Mahatma,* which means great soul.

Gandhi, Rajiv (1944–1991) Rajiv was Indira's oldest son. Voters elected him prime minister of India from 1984 to 1989. Until 1981 he worked as an airline pilot, then was elected to **parliament** and became a close adviser to his mother. Party members elected him prime minister and leader of the Congress I Party after the Sikhs assassinated Indira. He was assassinated in 1991.

Gandhi, Sanjay (1946–1980) Sanjay, Indira's younger son, became her closest political ally. In the state of emergency, Sanjay was responsible for two disastrous policies—family planning and slum clearance—that led to his mother's fall from power. He died in a plane crash in 1980.

Nehru, Jawaharlal (1889–1964) Nehru, Indira's father, served as the first prime minister of India from 1947 until his death in 1964. Educated at Harrow public school and Cambridge University in England, Nehru joined his father's legal practice in India and worked as a lawyer. After the Amritsar Massacre, he joined the independence movement and became a staunch supporter and close friend of Mohandas Gandhi. As a leader of the Indian National Congress, he spent much of Indira's childhood in jail.

Nehru, Motilal (1861–1931) Motilal, Indira's grandfather and father of Jawaharlal Nehru, came from a wealthy Kashmiri family. He settled in Allahabad, where he established a prosperous law practice. A follower of Western ways, he later gave up his law practice and became active in the independence movement.

Pandit, Vijayalakshmi (1900–1990) Pandit was Jawaharlal's sister and Indira's aunt. She played a prominent role in the independence movement and in the women's movement. In her political life, she served as Indian ambassador to the Soviet Union, the United States, Ireland, and Spain.

Shastri, Lal Bahadur (1904–1966) Shastri became prime minister of India in June 1964 after Jawaharlal Nehru's death. Born in Benares, Shastri entered politics after leaving college and joined the Indian National Congress in the 1920s. He was active in the independence movement, and the government jailed him several times. After independence, he served as the state of Uttar Pradesh's minister of police and transportation and later ran various ministries in the central government. He died in Tashkent, the capital of Uzbekistan, in January 1966, after signing a peace treaty with Pakistan.

Tagore, Rabindranath (1861–1941) Tagore was an Indian poet, novelist, playwright, philosopher, and painter. Born in Calcutta, he studied law in England then returned to India. In 1901 he established the Viswa Bharati University at Santiniketan in West Bengal as a center of universal learning. In 1913, he was awarded the Nobel Prize for literature. He wrote the national anthems of India, Bangladesh, and Sri Lanka. He supported Indian nationalism and, after the Amritsar massacre, he gave up the knighthood given to him by the British.

Sources for Further Research

Allen, Charles. *Soldier Sahibs: The Daring Adventurers Who Tamed India's Northwest Frontier.* Collingale, Pa.: Diane Publishing, 2001.

Bhashyam, Kasturi. *Walking Alone: Gandhi and India's Partition.* Delhi, India: Vision Publishing, 1999.

Dommermuth-Costa, Carol. *Indira Gandhi: Daughter of India.* Minneapolis, Minn.: Lerner Publications, 2001.

Downing, David. *Mohandas Gandhi.* Chicago: Heinemann Library, 2002.

Fisher, David and Read, Anthony. *The Proudest Day: India's Long Road to Independence.* New York: W. W. Norton and Co., 1999.

Furbee, Mike. *Mohandas Gandhi.* Farmington Hills, Mich.: Gale Group, 2000.

Malaspina, Anna. *Mahatma Gandhi and India's Independence in World History.* Berkeley Heights, N.J.: Enslow Publishers, Inc., 2000.

Resling, Darlene E. *Gandhi: A Play.* Baltimore, Md.: Learning Well, 1997.

Subramanian, S. *50 Years of India's Independence.* Delhi, India: Manas Publications, 1998.

Glossary

ancestor relative who died a long time ago

boycott refuse to buy or use something

cabinet group of senior politicians who lead the government

caste one of the four classes or groups into which Hindu society is traditionally divided

censor to remove material from books, movies, art, or other forms of communication that is considered to be morally or politically harmful

civil war war between different groups of people living in the same country

Congress Party leading political party of India for most of the time since independence. It began as the Indian National Congress in 1885.

corruption in politics, dishonesty, such as taking bribes

democracy form of government in which a country's people vote for their leaders

dictator ruler who does not allow ordinary people to have any say in how their country is governed

drought long period of time during which no rain falls

dynasty series of rulers belonging to the same family

exaltation feeling of great happiness or joy

famine a time when food is in short supply, and people are starving

fortitude great strength and courage

freedom fighters people who fight and struggle to help their country gain independence

Gandhi cap white, peaked cap worn by Mohandas Gandhi and his followers

Hindi one of the most widely spoken languages in India

Hindu follower of Hinduism, or the Hindu religion, which began in India and is still widely practiced there

industrial unrest when workers go on strike, stores and factories close, and transportation systems do not run

interim government government that fills in for a short time until a permanent government is elected

invigorate make someone feel more lively or energetic

khadi type of rough, homespun cloth

legislative assemblies parts of a country's government that make and pass laws

massacre brutal or violent killing of a large number of people

militant person who speaks out boldly or even commits violent acts in order to cause other people to support his or her beliefs

military dictatorship a form of government in which a country is ruled by a leader of the army or armed forces

monsoon heavy rains that fall in a certain part of the year. Farmers in some parts of the world rely on monsoons for watering their crops.

mosque building in which Muslims meet to pray

Muslim follower of the religion of Islam, which is the second largest religion in India after Hinduism

nationalist person who believes that the peoples of the world are made up of distinct nations, each of which should have its own country

nationalize change the ownership and control of industries or businesses from private hands to control by the government

parliament a group of elected leaders that make a country's laws (see box on page 33)

parochialism narrow-minded view

Parsi follower of the Zoroastrian religion, which began in Persia about 3,000 years ago. A large Parsi community lives in western India.

prime minister the chief executive in a parliamentary type of government. The office is similar to that of the president in the U.S. government.

refugees people who have fled from their own country to another country because of war or another disaster

republic form of government in which the people or their elected politicians have power

ruthless having no compassion, pity, or mercy. Ruthless people will do anything to get their way no matter how much it hurts other people.

saffron yellowish-orange color that Indian religions believe is holy

sanatorium clinic that specializes in treating people with illnesses that last a long time and are hard to cure. In the past, tuberculosis was such an illness.

sari traditional dress worn by Indian women made from a long piece of cloth wound around the body

Sikh follower of the Sikh religion, which began in Punjab, India, in the 1500s

sit-in form of protest in which people sit in a public place and refuse to move

sterilize to make a person permanently unable to have children by performing an operation on him or her

terrorism campaign of violence, usually against ordinary citizens rather than military troops, designed to frighten them and force them to change their values or political systems

tuberculosis disease that affects the lungs

verandah open balcony or gallery built along the side of a house

viceroy official who governs a country in the name of another country's king, queen, or government

Vietnam War war fought between 1954 and 1975 between North and South Vietnam. After 1961, the United States fought in the war in support of the South Vietnamese.

Index